contents

5 Land so great
25 *Second amendment*
41 Family ties
52 *First amendment*
57 United we stand
72 *The service they gave*
80 September, never
88 *Flag for Freedom*
98 Pursuit of happiness
124 *Her workers*
138 God is Great

Land of the Free, Home of the Heart

HANK LIBERTY

*for her, all 3,797million
square miles of her*

"America is not just a country, it's an idea, a dream, and a place where the impossible can happen."

land so free

part one

In skies so vast, with wings unfurled,
The eagle soars, a symbol of the world,
A guardian of freedom, fierce and bold,
A tale of courage and stories untold.

Its keen eyes pierce the endless blue,
With vision clear, it seeks what's true,
A sentinel of liberty's domain,
In its mighty talons, hope remains.

With feathers touched by the sun's warm kiss,
It glides through the heavens, pure and bliss,
A creature of grace, power, and grace,
In the land of dreams, it finds its place.

In the eagle's flight, a message sent,
A reminder of freedom's testament,
A symbol of strength, from mountains to shore,
The eagle of freedom, forever we adore.

With outstretched wings, it soars on high,
In its shadow, dreams can touch the sky,
The eagle of freedom, a symbol so grand,
In the heart of the land where dreams expand.

In the land where dreams take flight so high,
Beneath the endless, starry sky,
There lies a place where freedoms bloom,
In the heart of the USA's room.

From sea to shining sea, it spans,
A tapestry of diverse lands,
With liberty as its guiding light,
A beacon through the darkest night.

In the USA, the people say,
"We hold these truths, come what may,
That all are equal, in every way,
And justice must forever stay."

From Independence's bold decree,
To struggles for equality,
The fight for freedom marches on,
In the land where it was born.

In the USA, a dream was sown,
Where every voice has a chance to be known,
Where differences are celebrated with pride,
And together, we'll always stride.

So let us cherish this land so free,
A symbol of hope and liberty,
In the USA, where dreams take flight,
With freedom's flame, burning bright.

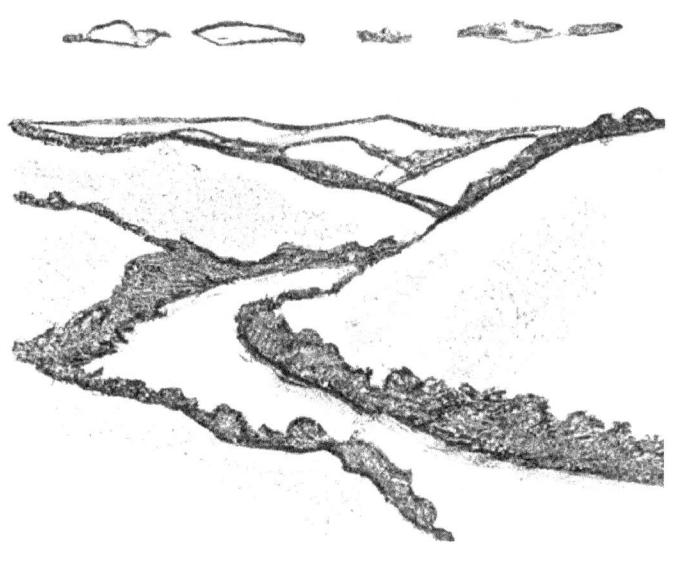

From sea to shining sea, a land so vast,
The United States, a beauty unsurpassed.
Its landscapes diverse, a stunning array,
In nature's grandeur, we find our way.

In the East, where the sun first greets the morn,
The Appalachian hills are gently worn.
With forests deep and rivers wide,
A tranquil beauty, where peace resides.

Midwest fields of golden grain,
Stretching wide on the endless plain.
Amidst the heartland's amber waves,
A sense of freedom softly engraves.

To the South, where magnolias bloom,
Cypress swamps and warm sun's loom.
A culture rich, steeped in history,
A land of charm and mystery.

Out West, the Rockies touch the sky,
Snow-capped peaks that reach up high.
Deserts vast, with colors bold,
A rugged beauty, a sight to behold.

In the North, the Great Lakes gleam,
A watery world, like a waking dream.
Forests dense and pristine air,
A paradise for those who dare.

From the Pacific coastline's crashing waves,
To the rolling hills of the heartland's graves,
The United States, a land so grand,
A masterpiece crafted by nature's hand.

In every corner, beauty thrives,
A testament to the land's rich lives.
From mountain peak to ocean shore,
The USA's landscapes we'll forever adore.

In fifty states, our nation stands so free,
A tapestry of dreams and liberty.
From the East Coast's dawn in Maine's embrace,
To Hawaii's sunset, a tranquil place.

In Alabama's heart, where history's told,
Through crimson leaves in Vermont's forests old.
From Florida's shores, where the sun does gleam,
To the mountains tall in Tennessee.

Kentucky's bluegrass, a peaceful sight,
Mississippi's river flows in gentle might.
Colorado's peaks, where eagles soar,
Nevada's desert, forever explored.

In Oregon's woods, the tall trees sway,
New York's skyline, where dreams hold sway.
From North Dakota's plains, so vast and grand,
To Arizona's desert, a fiery land.

Wisconsin's lakes, where waters flow,
Minnesota's North Star, a guiding glow.
Texas, where everything's big and bold,
Louisiana's bayou, where stories are told.

In the heart of Illinois, where cities thrive,
And in Rhode Island, where history's alive.
Connecticut's charm, where rivers meander,
In New Jersey's embrace, where dreams do wander.

Delaware's beauty, so quiet and serene,
Idaho's wilderness, a tranquil scene.
Montana's grandeur, where nature calls,
Utah's red rocks, where wonder enthralls.

In Oklahoma's plains, where winds do blow,
Arkansas's forests, where wildflowers grow.
Washington's evergreens, a majestic view,
And in South Carolina, skies so blue.

Georgia's peaches, so sweet to taste,
In Maryland's harbor, where ships are embraced.
Michigan's lakes, where waters are wide,
And in Wyoming's vastness, our spirits ride.

New Mexico's culture, a blend so rich,
Kansas' plains, where the wheat fields pitch.
Nebraska's heart, where dreams take hold,
And in Iowa's fields, where stories are told.

West Virginia's mountains, where adventure begins,
New Hampshire's woods, where the sunlight dims.
In South Dakota's Badlands, a rugged sight,
And in North Carolina's beauty, we find our light.

From Alaska's glaciers to the Great Lakes' shore,
In each of these states, freedom we adore.
United we stand, in diversity's grace,
In fifty states strong, our nation's embrace.

second amendment

part two

Right to bear arms strong,
Second Amendment's lifelong song,
Freedom's guard lifelong.

Muskets and today,
Second Amendment's display,
Debate holds its sway.

*Armed for self-defense,
Second Amendment's recompense,
Influence immense.*

*Individual right,
Second Amendment's insight,
Controversy's fight.*

Balancing the scale,
Second Amendment's detail,
Rights, but without fail.

With freedom's great trust,
Second Amendment's robust,
Debate, we discuss.

Right to self-defense,
Second Amendment's presence,
Freedom's recompense.

*Armed to protect life,
Second Amendment is rife,
With our rights so rife.*

Individual's right,
Second Amendment's birthright,
In liberty's light.

Guarding freedoms vast,
Second Amendment holds fast,
A right unsurpassed.

Balance we must find,
Second Amendment defined,
In the rights assigned.

With responsibility,
Second Amendment's decree,
A right, and duty.

*In the land of the brave and free,
The right to bear arms, a legacy,
A principle forged through history's might,
A guardian of liberty's sacred light.*

*With arms in hand, we stand secure,
Against threats that may obscure,
The values for which our nation strives,
In defense of our precious lives.*

But with this right comes great responsibility,
To use our arms with due civility,
For liberty demands a measured hand,
To protect, not harm, our fellow man.

In the pursuit of justice, we must tread,
With respect for the lives that lie ahead,
To cherish the freedoms we hold dear,
With empathy and conscience clear.

So let us honor this right we bear,
With wisdom, prudence, and utmost care,
For in the balance of this solemn art,
We find the essence of a nation's heart.

*Arms in freedom's name,
A right with great weight and aim,
Responsibility.*

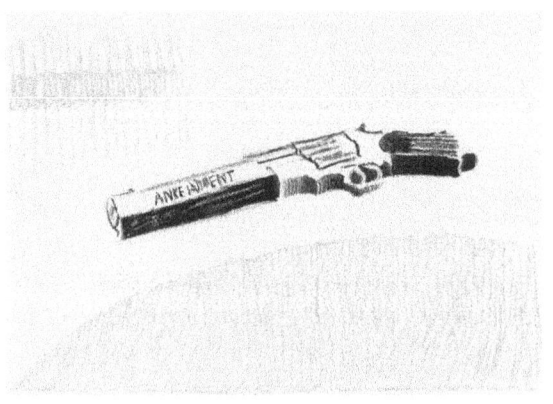

*In the people's trust,
Right to bear arms, we discuss,
Balance is a must.*

*Liberty's embrace,
Right to bear arms in our space,
With care, we replace.*

*Protecting the home,
Right to bear arms, we're shown,
With power comes responsibility grown.*

Armed for self-defense,
Right to bear arms, our recompense,
A nation's defense.

family ties

part three

*In the tapestry of life, a thread so true,
Is family, a bond like morning's dew.
With roots that run deep, like ancient trees,
They anchor us in life's wildest seas.*

*Through trials and triumphs, they stand beside,
In their embrace, we find a place to hide.
With laughter, love, and tears to share,
Family's the answer to every prayer.*

*In times of joy, they magnify the delight,
In moments of darkness, they are the light.
A source of strength, unwavering and strong,
In their presence, we truly belong.*

*They shape our values, teach us to be,
The best versions of ourselves, you see.
Through generations, their legacy lives,
The boundless love that family gives.*

*No matter where the winds of life may blow,
Family's the constant, the love that we know.
In their embrace, we find our peace,
For family's love will never cease.*

Family's warm embrace,
Love's bond in every embrace,
A treasured embrace.

*In laughter and tears,
Family's love through all the years,
A lifeline so dear.*

*Through thick and through thin,
In our hearts, they're kith and kin,
Family, our win.*

In times of despair,
Family's strength is always there,
A love beyond compare.

*In moments we share,
Family's love beyond compare,
Together, we care.*

In the quiet of the early morn,
A miracle of life is born,
A baby's cry, a joyful sound,
In that moment, love is found.

Tiny fingers, tiny toes,
A future filled with dreams and hopes,
Innocence in every gaze,
A precious gift, in many ways.

Life's journey just begun,
A new chapter, a rising sun,
With each breath, a chance to be,
The best that one can ever see.

- a celebration of life

*In the cradle of the mother's love,
A miracle descends from above,
A baby's laughter, pure and bright,
A beacon in the darkest night.*

A testament to life's grand design,
A chance to cherish and redefine,
The future in those sparkling eyes,
A world of endless, boundless skies.

With each new birth, we celebrate,
The wonder of life, it's not too late,
To welcome with open arms and heart,
A brand new life, a fresh start.

The Gift of New Beginnings

first amendment

part four

*Speech, press, religion,
First Amendment's protection,
Freedom's cornerstone.*

*Words like flowing streams,
First Amendment's sacred dreams,
In America's seams.*

*Voices rise and soar,
First Amendment, we adore,
Freedom to explore.*

*Opinions diverse,
First Amendment, we rehearse,
In liberty's verse.*

*In words, we unite,
First Amendment's guiding light,
Freedom's sacred right.*

united we stand

part five

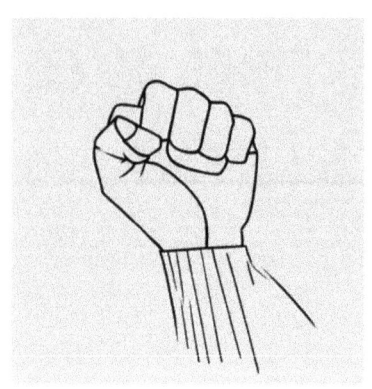

Rise, people, unite,
Protect our land's sacred light,
In freedom's brave fight.

United, we stand,
Guardians of our homeland,
With strength, hand in hand.

*In times of distress,
We the people, will address,
Protecting with finesse.*

*Vigilance our guide,
In our hearts, courage won't hide,
United, side by side.*

*A nation's call clear,
Rising up without fear,
Protecting what's dear.*

*With resolve we'll rise,
In freedom's boundless skies,
A nation's soul, wise.*

*In unity strong,
We'll prove that we belong,
In freedom's lifelong song.*

*A nation's defense,
In unity, we dispense,
Fear and recompense*

*Rising to protect,
Our values we won't neglect,
With strength, we'll connect.*

*In America's name,
We the people, rise to claim,
Our freedom's true aim.*

*The call to rise, a sacred creed,
In America's hour of need,
We the people, in unity,
Will safeguard our nation, forever
be free.*

-the call to rise

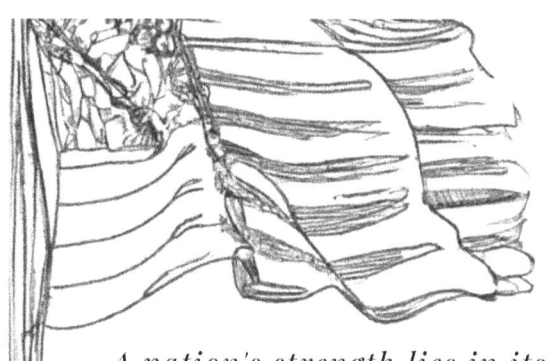

*A nation's strength lies in its might,
With vigilance, we'll win the fight,
To protect the values that we hold dear,
In the United States, there's no room for fear.*

-a nation's vigilance

*In times of trial, we must be bold,
Together as one, in the stories of old,
For the United States, we'll take a stand,
To safeguard our future, hand in hand.*

-united we stand

*As guardians of liberty, we rise,
With resolve in our hearts, reaching for the skies,
In the face of challenges, we unite,
To protect our freedoms, with all our might.*

-we are the guardians of liberty

In unity we stand, a nation's call,
To protect the land, we give our all,
We the people, strong and true,
In defense of the red, white, and blue

-Rise, O People

*In unity's might,
We defend what's just and right,
Freedom's guiding light.*

*Oppression's dark scheme,
Together, we'll never deem,
For freedom, we dream.*

United we stand,
Against those who would demand,
Our freedom, hand in hand.

In shadows cast by towering walls,
Where power reigns and freedom falls,
A voice emerges, strong and clear,
To question what we hold so dear.

For governments, they often claim,
To serve the people, but is it the same?
When secrecy and corruption breed,
It's time for truth to take the lead.

In corridors of hidden might,
Decisions made, out of sight,
The people's voice, it can be drowned,
In a system where power is tightly wound.

Yet, let us not just blindly rage,
But seek to turn a brighter page,
Demand transparency and rights,
To hold the powerful to the light.

For governments, they're meant to serve,
The people's needs they must observe,
But when they fail to do what's right,
It's our duty to question, to fight.

So let us strive for a world more just,
In which the people can truly trust,
That government's role is clear and true,
To serve the many, not just the few.

the service they gave

part six

Home from far-off lands,
Bravery in their strong hands,
Heroes among us.

They fought for our peace,
In their hearts, the battles cease,
Grateful hearts find ease.

Veterans return,
With valor, they proudly serve,
Salute their courage.

*In uniforms of courage, they stand tall,
Answering the nation's noble call,
Soldiers, heroes, brave and true,
Defending freedom, red, white, and blue.*

*Through trials and battles, they march on,
With hearts of bravery, strong and drawn,
They bear the weight of freedom's plea,
In service to a land so proud and free.*

*In far-off lands, they take their stand,
Protecting home, their homeland,
With sacrifice and honor, they serve,
Deserving all the honor they've earned.*

-soldiers valor

In the silent watches of the night,
Soldiers stand, their duty right,
Guardians of peace, in lands afar,
Defending freedom, no matter how far.

Through hardship, they find their strength,
With honor and courage, they go to great lengths,
A selfless service, a noble creed,
In the name of justice, they always lead.

*Their stories told in deeds and grace,
Soldiers, warriors, in every place,
For in their service, heroes rise,
A testament to the skies so wise.*

September never

part seven

In skies so blue, that fateful morn,
A day when innocence was torn,
September 11, etched in pain,
Our world would never be the same.

*Twin towers kissed by morning light,
A symbol of New York's towering might,
But terror struck with ruthless force,
Changing the course of our life's course.*

*Through smoke and ash, heroes rose,
In the face of fear, their courage shows,
First responders, hearts of steel,
They ran toward danger, not away to heal.*

*In unity, we stood as one,
A nation under the morning sun,
Remembering those we lost that day,
And the strength that helped us find our way.*

On September 11, the world did weep,
As shadows o'er the skyline swept,
A day of terror, pain, and sorrow,
We vowed to face a new tomorrow.

*The towers fell, but not our spirit,
In the face of hate, we chose to bear it,
With hearts united, we would stand,
Together, hand in hand.*

In the darkness, heroes shone,
Their bravery like a beacon, known,
First responders, and those who gave,
Their lives to help, to heal, to save.

*We'll never forget the lives we lost,
Or the countless lines that love has crossed,
In their memory, we'll forever strive,
To keep their spirit and hope alive.*

Flag for freedom

part eight

*A flag of red and white,
With stars that shine so bright,
A symbol of freedom's might,
The Stars and Stripes in flight.*

Old Glory, proudly wave,
Over land of the free, the brave,
In your colors, we find unity,
A symbol of our liberty.

In the dawn's early light,
The flag's colors take flight,
A proud symbol, standing tall,
A nation's anthem for all.

In the land of hopes and dreams,
The flag's beauty gleams,
A reminder of the sacrifices made,
For the freedoms that will never fade.

Through battles fought, in the darkest night,
The flag endured, a steadfast sight,
A beacon of hope, a nation's pride,
In Old Glory, we confide.

Stripes and stars on high,
Old Glory against the sky,
Freedom's banner fly.

Red, white, blue unite,
In the flag's colors, the fight,
For justice takes flight.

Stars twinkle and gleam,
In the flag, a timeless dream,
Liberty's sunbeam.

Flag waves in the breeze,
Whispers of freedom it sees,
Land of the brave, please.

*In each fold and seam,
The American dream,
The flag's eternal theme.*

pursuit of happiness

part nine

The American Dream

*In the land of dreams and endless skies,
Where hopes take flight, and ambition lies,
The American Dream, a guiding light,
A promise that shines through day and night.*

Pursuit of the Dream

*Through sweat and toil, with hearts aflame,
We chase our dreams, and they become our name,
In the USA, where dreams find a place,
The American Dream we eagerly embrace.*

Dreams in Red, White, and Blue

From every corner of the world, we come,
To build a life, to make a home,
In the USA, where dreams can come true,
The American Dream, for me and for you.

In Dreams We Trust

In the American Dream, we believe,
A vision of hope that we all achieve,
With freedom and opportunity, we aspire,
In the land where dreams catch fire.

Dreams in Every Heart

In each heart that beats, a dream resides,
In the USA, where hope abides,
The American Dream, a journey's start,
In the land of dreams, it's in every heart.

Dreams bloom, red, white, blue,
In the land where skies are true,
American dream.

*Opportunity,
In the American sea,
Dreams set sail so free.*

*In the USA,
Where dreams have their grand display,
Hope lights up the way.*

*In dreams we believe,
In the land where hopes conceive,
American dream.*

*In each heart that beats,
American dreams take their seats,
In the land so sweet.*

Dreams take flight, they soar,
In the USA's grand tour,
Land of dreams and more.

Opportunity,
In the land of liberty,
American dream.

*From near and afar,
Dreamers follow their North Star,
In the USA.*

In the land so vast,
Dreams are built to forever last,
American dream.

In freedom's embrace,
The American Dream we chase,
In this sacred place.

Chasing Happiness

*In the pursuit of happiness, we roam,
Through valleys low and mountains' foam,
A journey filled with joy and grace,
As we seek that elusive happy place.*

Happiness Unveiled

Happiness, a treasure sought,
In every life, a dream caught,
In the laughter of a child's delight,
In the warmth of a starry night.

Pursuing Joy

With each sunrise, a chance to find,
The happiness that fills the mind,
In the simplest moments, it's found,
In the beauty of the world around.

The Pursuit's Reward

In the pursuit of happiness, we strive,
Through every challenge, we come alive,
For happiness, the ultimate prize,
In its embrace, our spirit flies.

The Quest for Bliss

In the endless quest for happiness we roam,
Through life's twists and turns, we find our home,
In the heart's contentment and love's sweet kiss,
We discover the essence of true happiness.

Chasing happiness,
In life's grand, unfolding quest,
Joy is our compass.

*In each sunrise's glow,
The pursuit of joy we know,
Happiness to sow.*

Happiness, a song,
In every heart, it belongs,
Life's sweet, endless throng.

Seeking happiness,
Through life's joys and
hardships' stress,
In our hearts, it rests.

In the starry night,
Happiness, a guiding light,
In dreams, taking flight.

In laughter and cheer,
Happiness is always near,
In each moment, clear.

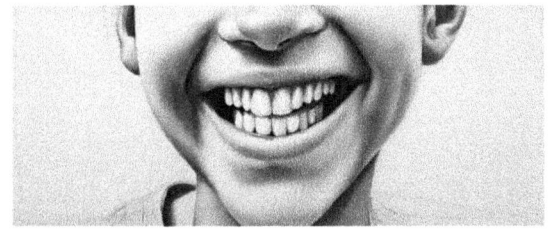

Pursuit of delight,
Happiness takes its own flight,
In life's sweet twilight.

*In love's sweet embrace,
Happiness finds its own place,
In every warm trace.*

*Chasing happiness,
Through the years of
toil and stress,
In joy, we confess.*

*In the heart's deep
quest,
Happiness is truly best,
In life's warmest nest.*

her workers

part ten

The Working Class Heroes

*In factories, farms, and city streets,
Working class Americans meet,
The backbone of the land so vast,
Their toil and sweat, a strength that lasts.*

Builders of the Nation

With calloused hands and hearts so true,
They build the dreams that we pursue,
The working class, a sturdy band,
The ones who truly understand.

America's Foundation

From dawn till dusk, they pave the way,
With every sunrise, a new day,
The working class, in shadows cast,
A vital role, from first to last.

Strength in Unity

In unity, they stand as one,
Their work, the work that must be done,
The working class, a beacon bright,
Guiding us through day and night.

The Heartbeat of the Nation

*In their sweat and in their tears,
The working class conquers fears,
The heartbeat of the nation strong,
In their dedication, we all belong.*

Working class, so strong,
Backbone of the land we're on,
Their dreams carry on.

Hands calloused with care,
Working class, always there,
Strength beyond compare.

*In factories they toil,
Working class, a tireless coil,
Their worth, a royal.*

*From dawn's early light,
Working class, a steadfast sight,
Guiding us through night.*

Builders of the land,
Working class, hand in hand,
United, they stand.

In every city's heart,
Working class plays a part,
Their role, a true art.

*In sweat and in toil,
Working class, the fertile soil,
Dreams begin to uncoil.*

*Strength in unity,
Working class, community,
Their pride, our affinity.*

In the heart of the land,
Working class, a helping hand,
They truly understand.

America's soul,
Working class, reaching their goal,
Their worth makes us whole.

god is great

part eleven

Sunday's gentle call,
To the church we gather all,
Faith's embrace enthralls.

Beneath the stained glass,
Prayers and hymns together pass,
In God's love, we amass.

Bells ring in the air,
In the pews, we kneel in prayer,
Grace and hope we share.

*Fellowship and song,
In the church, we all belong,
God's love, forever strong.*

God's wisdom above,
In faith, we find endless love,
Heavenly dove.

In God's loving grace,
Strength and solace we embrace,
Guiding every pace.

In God, we confide,
In our hearts, faith does reside,
In Him, we abide.

In the beauty of belief, a message to share,
A collection of poems, a heartfelt affair.
In the verses to come, the Lord we'll adore,
With words of devotion, we'll praise Him even more.

Stay tuned for the poems, a spiritual delight,
To celebrate the Lord, His love shining bright.
In poetry, we'll find His grace and His word,
A collection of verses, in His name, to be heard.

-Hank

*Coming in 2024 – a collection of
poetry devoted to our lord*

Land Of The Free, Home Of The Heart
Copyright © 2023 Hank Liberty. All right reserved. No part of this book may be used or reproduced in any manner whatsoever without the written permission except in the case of reprints in the context of reviews.

Patriot Pages Publishing
PO Box 2005
Armstrong Creek, Victoria
Australia 3217

www.patriotpagespublishing.com

Illustrations and cover design by Hank Liberty

Digital production: Ed Molnar

www.ingramcontent.com/pod-product-compliance
Lightning Source LLC
Chambersburg PA
CBHW040742020526
44107CB00084B/2839